Expert Systems and Expert Support Systems

EXPERT SYSTEMS AND EXPERT SUPPORT SYSTEMS: THE NEXT CHALLENGE FOR MANAGEMENT

Fred L. Luconi
Thomas W. Malone
Michael S. Scott Morton

90s: 85-005

Working Paper

Management in the 1990s

Massachusetts Institute of Technology
Sloan School of Management

EXPERT SYSTEMS AND EXPERT
SUPPORT SYSTEMS
THE NEXT CHALLENGE
FOR MANAGEMENT

Fred L. Luconi
Thomas W. Malone
Michael S. Scott Morton

90s 85-005

December, 1984
(Revised September, 1985)

CISR WP #122
Sloan WP #1630-85

A version of this paper appears in Sloan Management Review, Fall 1986 (forthcoming), and in
The Rise of Managerial Computing The Best of the Center for Information Systems Research,
J F Rockart and C V Bullen, eds., Dow Jones Irwin, Homewood Illinois 1986

Management in the 1990s
Sloan School of Management
Massachusetts Institute of Technology

Management in the 1990s is an industry and governmental agency supported research program Its aim is to develop a better understanding of the managerial issues of the 1990s and how to deal most effectively with them, particularly as these issues revolve around anticipated advances in Information Technology

Assisting the work of the Sloan School scholars with financial support and as working partners in research are

American Express Travel Related Services Company
Arthur Young and Company
British Petroleum Company, p l c
BellSouth Corporation
Digital Equipment Corporation
Eastman Kodak Company
General Motors Corporation
International Computers, Ltd
MCI Communications Corporation
United States Internal Revenue Service

The conclusions or opinions expressed in this paper are those of the author(s) and do not necessarily reflect the opinion of Massachussetts Institute of Technology, Management in the 1990s Research Program, or its sponsoring organizations

In this age of the "microchip revolution" effective managers are finding ways to learn and profitably use the myriad applications of the silicon chip. These applications include personal computers, office automation, robotics, computer graphics, and the various forms of broad band and narrow band communication. One of the most intriguing of these new applications to emerge from the research labs and move into the practical world of business is Expert Systems (E.S.). Most literature about Expert Systems describes the technical concepts upon which they are based and the small number of systems already in use.

In this article we shift this focus and discuss how these systems can be used in a broad range of business applications. We will argue that in many business applications, the knowledge that can be feasibly encoded in an Expert System is not sufficient to make satisfactory decisions by itself. Instead, we believe that our focus should increasingly be on designing Expert Support Systems (E.S.S.) that will aid, rather than replace, human decision makers.

After briefly defining a few Expert Systems concepts, we offer an expansion of a classical framework for understanding managerial problem-solving. We then use this framework to identify limitations of many current expert systems and decision support systems and show how expert support systems can be seen as the next logical step in both fields.

BASIC CONCEPTS

Winston (19) defines Artificial Intelligence (AI) as " the study of ideas which enable computers to do the things that make people seem intelligent" (page 1). In order to do this AI systems attempt to deal with qualitative as well quantitative information, ambiguous and "fuzzy" reasoning and rules of thumb that give good but not always optimal solutions.

Another way of characterizing artificial intelligence is not in terms of what it attempts to do, but in terms of the programming techniques and philosophies it has evolved. We will give examples below of specfic techniques such as "frames" and "rules" that allow AI programmers to represent knowledge in ways that are often much more flexible and much more natural for humans to deal with than the algorithimic procedures   used in traditional programming languages.

In spite of a great deal of early over-optimism in the field of artificial intelligence, there are at least three areas in which AI, in its current state of development, appears to have promising near term applications: robotics, natural language understanding, and expert systems. In this article, we will focus on the realistic potentials for the use of expert systems in business. In order to emphasize our main point about appropriate ways of using these systems we will exaggerate a distinction between expert systems, as they are often conceived, and a variation of expert systems we will call Expert Support Systems.

Expert Systems

Expert Systems techniques can be used to preserve and disseminate scarce expertise by encoding the relevant experience of an expert and making this expertise available as a resource to the less expert. For example, the Schlumberger Corporation uses its 'Dipmeter Advisor' to access the interpretive abilities of a handful of their most productive geological experts and make it available to their field geologists all over the world (16). The program takes oil well log data about the geological characteristics of a well and makes inferences about the probable location of oil in that region.

Expert systems can also be used to solve problems that thwart traditional programming techniques. For example, another early system in practical use is known as XCON. Developed at Digital Equipment Corporation in a joint effort with Carnegie-Mellon University, XCON uses some 3300 rules and 5500 product descriptions to configure the specific detailed components of VAX and other computer systems in response to the customers' overall orders. The system first determines what, if any, substitutions and additions have to be made to the order so that it is complete and consistent and then this system produces a number of diagrams showing the electrical connections and room layout for the 50-150 components in a typical system (4).

This application was attempted unsuccessfully several times using traditional programming techniques before the A.I. effort was initiated. The system has been in daily use now for over four years and the savings have been substantial, not only in terms of the

technical editor's scarce time, but also in ensuring that no
component is missing at installation time, an occurrence that delays
the customer's acceptance of the system (12).

A second factor making A.I. applications, such as Expert
Systems, feasible today is the development of programming tools for
nonspecialists that are capable of supporting symbol manipulation
and incremental development. These facilities permit one to
prototype, experiment and modify as required and have resulted in
"Power Tools for Programmers" (14) -- environments of significantly
greater potential than those usually provided by traditional data
processing resources.

Definitions

With these examples in mind we can now define Expert Systems as
follows·

Expert Systems - computer programs that use specialized symbolic
reasoning to solve difficult problems well.

In other words Expert Systems: (1) use specialized knowledge
about a particular problem area (such as geological analysis or
computer configuration) rather than just general purpose knowledge
that would apply to all problems, (2) use symbolic (and often
qualitative) reasoning rather than just numerical calculations, and
(3) perform at a level of competence that is better than that of
non-expert humans.

Expert Support Systems use all these same techniques but focus
on helping people solve the problems:

Expert Support Systems - computer programs that use specialized
symbolic reasoning to help people solve difficult problems well.

-4-

Expert Support Systems

E.S.S. (Expert Support Systems) take E.S. techniques and apply them to a much wider class of problems than is possible with pure expert systems. They do this by pairing the human with the expert system, thus creating a joint decision process in which the human is the dominant partner, providing overall problem-solving direction as well as specific knowledge not incorporated in the system. Some of this knowledge can be thought of beforehand and made explicit, thus becoming embedded in the expert system. However, much of the knowledge may be imprecise and will remain below the level of consciousness, to be recalled to the conscious level of the decision-maker only when triggered by the evolving problem context.

Heuristic Reasoning

One of the most important ways in which expert systems differ from traditional computer applications is in their use of heuristic reasoning. Traditional applications are completely understood and therefore can employ algorithms, that is, precise rules that, when followed, lead to the correct conclusion. For example, the amount of a payroll check for an employee is calculated according to a precise set of rules. Expert Systems use heuristic techniques. An heuristic system involves judgemental reasoning, trial and error and therefore is appropriate for more complex problems. The heuristic decision rules or inference procedures generally provide a good-but not necessarily optimum-answer.

Problems appropriate for A.I. techniques are those that cannot be solved algorithmically; that is, by precise rules. The problems are either too large, such as the possibilities encountered in the game of chess, or too imprecise, such as the diagnosis of a particular person's medical condition.

Components of Expert Systems

To understand in more detail how expert systems (and expert support systems) are different from traditional computer applications, it is important to understand what the components of a typical expert system are (See Figure 1). In addition to the user interface for communicating with a human user, a typical expert system also has (1) a knowledge base of facts and rules related to the problem and (2) an inference engine or reasoning methods for using the

information in the knowledge base to solve problems. Separating
these two components makes it much easier to change the system as
the problem changes or becomes better understood. For example, new
rules can be added to the knowledge base, one by one, in such a way
that all the old facts and reasoning methods can still be used. To
give a flavor of the kinds of techniques that characterize AI we
will briefly describe some elements of these systems in more detail.

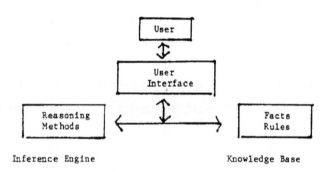

Inference Engine   Knowledge Base

Expert System Architecture

Figure 1

Knowledge Base

In order to flexibly use specialized knowledge about many
different kinds of problems, A.I. researchers have developed a
number of new "knowledge representation" techniques. Using these
techniques to provide structure for a body of knowledge is still
very much an art, and is practiced by an emerging group of
professionals known as "knowledge engineers". Knowledge engineers

in this field are akin to the systems analysts of Data Processing (D.P.) applications. They work with the 'experts' and draw out the relevant expertise in a form that can be encoded in a computer program. Three of the most important techniques for encoding this knowledge are (1) production rules, (2) semantic nets, and (3) frames.

Production Rules. Production rules are particularly useful in building systems based on heuristic methods (17). These are simple "if-then" rules that are often used to represent the empirical consequences of a given condition: or the action that should be taken in a given situation. For example, a medical diagnosis system might have a rule like

If 1) The patient has fever, and

   2) The patient has a runny nose

Then: it is very likely (.9) that

       the patient has a cold.

A computer configuration system might have a rule like

If 1) There is an unassigned single port disk drive, and

   2) There is a free controller,

Then: Assign the disk drive to the controller port.

Semantic Nets. Another formalism that is often more convenient than production rules for representing certain kinds of relational knowledge is called "semantic networks" or "semantic nets." For example, in order to apply the rule about assigning disk drives that was shown above, a system would need to know what part numbers coresponded to single port disk drives, controllers, and so forth.

Figure 2 shows how this knowledge might be represented in a network
of "nodes" connected by "links" that signify which classes of
components are subsets of other classes.

SEMANTIC NETWORKS

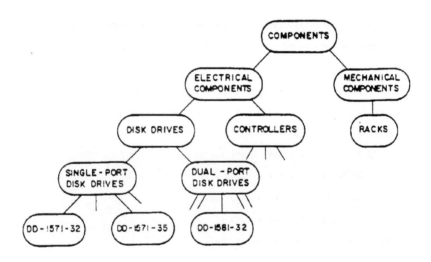

Figure 2

Frames. In many cases, it is convenient to gather into one
place a number of different kinds of information about an object.
For example, Figure 3 shows how several dimensions (such as length,

width, and power requirements) that describe electrical components might be represented as different "slots" in a "frame" about electrical components. Unlike traditional records in a data base, frames often contain additional features such as "default values" and "attached procedures." For example, if the default value for voltage requirement of an electrical component is 110 volts then the system would infer that a new electrical component required 110 volts unless explicit information to the contrary was provided. An attached procedure might automatically update the "volume" slot, whenever "length," "height," or "width" are changed.

Frames

Electrical Component	
Part No.	
Length	
Width	
Height	
Volume	
Voltage	

Figure 3

These three knowledge representation techniques, production
rules, semantic nets, and frames, have considerable power as they
permit us to capture knowledge in a way that can be exploited by the
'inference engine' to produce good, workable answers to the
questions at hand.

Inference Engine

The inference engine contains the reasoning methods that might
be used by human problem solvers when attacking problems. As these
are separate from the knowledge base it permits either to be changed
relatively independent of the other. Two reasoning methods often
employed with production rules are <u>forward chaining</u> and <u>backward</u>
<u>chaining</u>. Imagine, for instance, that we have a set of production
rules like those shown in Figure 4 for a personal financial planning
expert system. Imagine also that we know the current client's tax
bracket is 50%, nis liquidity is greater than $100,000, and he has a
high tolerance for risk. By forward chaining through the rules, one
at a time, tne system could infer that exploratory oil ana gas
investments should be recommended for this client. With a larger
rule base, many other investment recommendations might be deduced as
well.

Now imagine that we only want to know that whether exploratory
oil and gas investments are appropriate for a particular client and
we are not interested in any other investments at the moment. The
system can use exactly the same rule base to answer this specific
question more efficiently by "backward chaining" through the rules.

When backward chaining the system starts with a goal (e.g., "show
that this client needs exploratory oil and gas investments") and
asks at each stage what subgoals it would need to reach to achieve
this goal. For instance, in this example, to conclude that the
client needs exploratory oil and gas investments, we can use the
third rule if we know that risk tolerance is high (which we already
do know) and that a tax shelter is indicated. To conclude that a
tax shelter is indicated we have to find another rule (in this case,
the first one) and then check whether its conditions are satisfied.
In this case, they are, so our goal is achieved: we know we can
recommend exploratory oil and gas investments to this client.

FORWARD CHAINING

If   Tax bracket = 50%
       and liquidity is greater than $100,000

Then   A tax shelter is indicated.

If   A tax shelter is indicated
       and risk tolerance is low

Then   Recommend developmental oil
       and gas investments.

If   A tax shelter is indicated
       and risk tolerance is high

Then   Recommend exploratory oil
       and gas investments.

Backward Chaining
(Subgoaling)

What about exploratory oil and gas?

If   Tax bracket = 50%
       and liquidity is greater than $100,000

Then   A tax shelter is indicated.

If   A tax shelter is indicated
       and risk tolerance is low

Then   Recommend developmental oil
       and gas investments.

If   A tax shelter is indicated
       and risk tolerance is high

Then   Recommend exploratory oil
       and gas investments.

Figure 4

With these basic concepts in mind we turn now to a framework
that puts Expert Systems and Expert Support Systems into a
management context.

FRAMEWORK FOR EXPERT SUPPORT SYSTEMS

The framework developed below begins to allow us to identify
those classes of business problems that are appropriate for Data
Processing (D.P.), Decision Support Systems (D.S.S.), Expert Systems
(E.S.), and Expert Support Systems (E.S.S.). We can, in addition,
clarify the relative contributions of humans and computers in the
various classes of applications.

This framework extends the earlier work of Gorry and
Scott Morton, "Framework of Management Information Systems,"(8) in
which they relate Herbert Simon's seminal work on structured vs.
unstructured decision making (15) to Robert Anthony's strategic
planning, management control, and operational control (2). Figure 5
presents this original framework. Gorry and Scott Morton argued
that to improve the quality of decisions, the manager must seek not
only to match the type and quality of information and its
presentation to the category of decision, but also to choose a
system that reflects the degree of the problem's structure.

	Strategic Planning	Management Control	Operational Control
Structured			
Semi-Structured			
Unstructured			

Figure 5

With the benefit of experience in building and using Decisio
Support Systems, and in light of the insights garnered from the
field of Artificial Intelligence, it is useful to expand and ret
the structured/unstructured dimension of the original framework.
Simon nad broken down decision making into three phases,
Intelligence, Design and Choice. A structured decision was one
where all three phases were fully understood and "computable" by
human decision maker. As a result they could be programmed. In
unstructured decisions, one or more of these phases was not full
understood.

We can extend this distinction by taking Alan Newell's
insightful categorization of problem solving (13), as consisting
the following components:

Goals, Constraints; State Space; Search Control Knowledge, a
Operators.

In a business context, it seems helpful to relabel these pro
characteristics and group them into four categories:

1. Data - the dimensions and values necessary to represent
   state of the world that is relevant to the problem (i.e.
   the "state space")

2. Procedures - the sequences of steps (or "operators") use
   solving the problem.

3. Goals and Constraints - the desired results of problem
   solving and the constraints on what can and cannot be do

4. Strategies - the flexible strategies used in deciding wh
   procedures to apply to achieve goals (i.e. the "search
   control knowledge")

PROBLEM TYPES

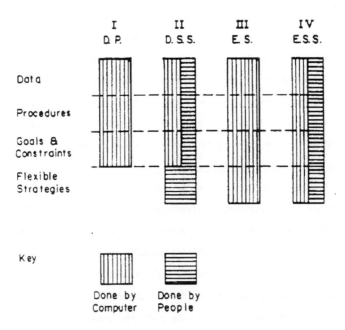

Figure 6

For some problems we can apply a standard procedure (i.e., an algorithm or formula) and proceed directly to a conclusion with no need for flexible problem-solving strategies. For example, we can use standard procedures to compute withholding taxes and prepare employee paychecks and we can use the classical economic order quantity formula to solve straightforward inventory control problems. In other cases a solution can be found only by identifying alternative approaches, and thinking through (in some cases via simulation) the effects of these alternative courses of action. One then chooses the approach that appears to create the best result. For example, to determine which of three sales strategies to use for a new product, a manager might want to explore the consequences of each for advertising expenses, sales force utilization, revenue, and so forth. In the remainder of this section we will discuss the range of these different types of problems and the appropriate kinds of systems for each.

Type I Problems - Data Processing

A fully structured problem is one in which all four of the elements of the problem are structured. That is, we have well stated goals, and we can specify the input data needed, and there are standard procedures by which a solution may be calculated. No complex strategies for generating and evaluating alternatives are needed. Fully structured problems are computable and one can decide if such computation is justifiable given the amounts of time and computing resource involved.

These problems are well suited to the use of conventional programming techniques. In conventional programming, virtually everything about the problem is well defined. In effect, the expert (i.e., the analyst/programmer) has already solved the problem. He or she must only sequence the data through the particular program.

Figure 6 represents pictorially the class of decision problems that
can be solved economically using conventional programming .
techniques. We will refer to this class as Type I problems,
problems historically thought of as ones suited for Data Processing

It is interesting to note that the economics of conventional
programming are being fundamentally altered with the provision of
new tools such as an "analyst's workbench." (14) These are
professional work stations used by the systems analyst to develop
flow chart representations of the problem and then move
automatically to testable, running code. The more advanced of these
stations happen to use A I. techniques, thus turning these new
techniques into tools to make our old approaches more effective in
classical D.P. application areas.

Type II Problems - Decision Support Systems

As we leave problems which are fully structured we begin to deal
with many of the problems organizations have to grapple with each
day. These are cases where standard procedures are helpful but not
sufficient by themselves, where the data may be incompletely
represented, and where the goals and constraints are only partially
understood. Traditional data processing systems do not solve these
problems. Fortunately, we have the possibility in these cases, of
letting the computer perform the well-understood parts of the
problem solving while relying on humans to use their goals,
intuition, and general knowledge to formulate problems, modify and
control the problem solving and interpret the results. As Figure 6

shows, the human users may provide or modify data, procedures or goals, and they may use their knowledge of all these factors to decide on problem-solving strategies.

In many of the best known Decision Support Systems (11) for example, the computer applies standard procedures to certain highly structured data but relies on the human users to decide which procedures are appropriate in a given situation and whether a given result is satisfactory or not. For example, the investment managers who used the portfolio management system (P.M.S.) (11) did not rely on the computer for either making final decisions about portfolio composition or for deciding on which procedures to use for analysis. They used the computer to execute the procedures they felt were appropriate, for example calculating portfolio diversity and expected returns, but the managers themselves proposed alternative portfolios and decided whether a given diversification or return was acceptable. Many people who use spreadsheet programs today for "what if" analyses follow a similar flexible strategy of proposing an action, letting the computer predict its consequences and then deciding what action to propose next.

Type III - Expert Systems

Using A.I. programming techniques like production rules and frames, expert systems are able to encode some of the same kinds of goals, heuristics, and strategies that people use in solving problems but that have previously been very difficult to use in computer programs. These techniques make it possible to design systems that don't just follow standard procedures, but instead use flexible problem-solving strategies to explore a number of possible alternatives before picking a solution.

For some cases, like the XCON system, these techniques can capture almost all the relevant knowledge about the problem. As of 1983, fewer than one out of every 1000 orders configured by XCON was misconfigured because of missing or incorrect rules. (Only about 10% of the orders had to be corrected for any reason at all and almost all of these errors were due to missing descriptions of rarely used parts (4).)

We call the problems where essentially all the relevant knowledge for flexible problem solving can be encoded Type III Problems. The systems that solve them are called Expert Systems.

It is instructive to note, however, that even with XCON—which is probably the most extensively tested system in commercial use today, new knowledge is continually being added and human editors still check every order the system configures. As the developers of XCON remark

> "There is no more reason to believe now than
> there was [in 1979] that [XCON] has all the
> knowledge relevant to its configuration task.
> This, coupled with the fact that [XCON] deals with
> an ever-changing domain implies its development
> will never be finished."
>
> (See 4, Page 27)

If XCON, which operates in the fairly restricted domain of computer order configuration, never contains all the knowledge relevant to its problem, it appears much less likely that we will ever be able to codify all the knowledge needed for less clearly bounded problems like financial analysis, strategic planning, and project management. Even in what might appear to be the fairly simple case of job shop scheduling, there are often very many continually changing and possibly implicit constraints on what people, machines, and parts are needed and available for different steps in a manufacturing process. (See 7.)

What this suggests is that for very many of the problems of practical importance in business we should focus our attention on designing systems that <u>support</u> expert users rather than replacing them.

Type IV - Expert Support Systems

Even in situations where important kinds of problem-solving knowledge, in all four areas of the problem cannot feasibly be encoded, it is still possible to use expert systems techniques. This dramatically extends the capabilities of computers beyond previous technologies such as D.P. and D.S.S.

What is important, in these cases, is to design Expert Support Systems (See Figure 6) with very good and deeply embedded "user interfaces" that enable their human users to easily inspect and control the problem-solving process. In other words, a good expert support system should be both <u>accessible</u> and <u>malleable</u>. Many expert support systems make their problem-solving accessible to users by providing explanation capabilities. For example, the MYCIN medical diagnosis program can explain to a doctor at any time why it is

asking for a given piece of information or what rules it used to
arrive at a given conclusion. For a system to be malleable, users
should be able to easily change data, procedures, goals, or
strategies at any important point in the problem-solving process.
Systems with this capability are still rare, but an early version of
the Dipmeter Advisor suggests how it might be provided (5). In this
version there was no satisfactory way to automatically detect
certain kinds of geological patterns, so human experts used a
graphical display of the data to mark and annotate these patterns.
The system then continued its analysis using this information.

An even more vivid example of how a system can be made
accessible and malleable is provided by the Steamer Program (See 10)
for teaching people to reason about operating a steam plant. This
system has colorful graphic displays of the schematic flows in the
simulated plant, the status of different valves and gauges, and the
pressures in different places. Users of the system can manipulate
these displays (using a "mouse" pointing device) to control the
valves, temperatures, and so forth. The system continually updates
its simulation results and expert diagnostics based on these user
actions.

Summary of Framework

This framework helps clarify a number of issues. First, it
highlights, as did the original Gorry and Scott Morton framework,
the importance of matching system type to problem type. In the

original 1971 article, however, the primary practical points to be made were that traditional D.P. technologies should not be used for semi-structured and unstructured problems where new D.S.S. technologies were more appropriate; secondly that interactive human/computer use opened up an extended class of problems where computers could be usefully exploited. The most important practical point to be made today is again two-fold: first, that "pure" expert systems should not be used for partially understood problems where expert support systems are more appropriate, and second that expert systems techniques can be used to dramatically extend the capabilities of traditional decision support systems.

Figure 3 shows, in an admittedly simplified way, how we can view expert support systems as the next logical step in each of two somewhat separate progressions. On the left side of the figure, we see that D.S.S. developed out of a practical recognition of the limits of D.P. for helping real human beings solve complex problems in actual organizations. The right side of the figure reflects a largely independent evolution that took place in computer science research laboratories and that developed from a recognition of the limits of traditional computer science techniques for solving the kinds of complex problems that people are able to solve. We are now at the point where these two separate progressions can be united to help solve a broad range of important practical problems.

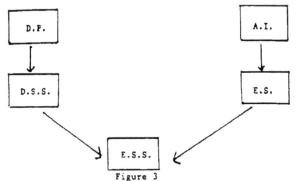

Figure 3
Progressions in Computer System Development

THE IMPORTANCE OF E.S.S. FOR MANAGEMENT

The real importance of E.S.S. lies in the ability of these
systems to harness and make full use of our scarcest resource: the
talent and experience of key members of the organization. There can
be considerable benefits in capturing the expert's experience and
making it available to those in an organization that are less expert
in the subject in question.

As organizations and their problems become more complex,
management can benefit from initiating prototype E.S. and E.S.S.'s.
The question now facing managers is when to start, and in which
areas.

The 'when' to start is relatively easy to answer. It is 'now'
for exploratory work. For some organizations this will be a program
of education and active monitoring of the field. For others the
initial investment may take the form of an experimental low budget

prototype. For a few, once the exploration is over, it will make good economic sense to go forward with a full-fledged working prototype. Conceptual and technological developments have made it possible to begin an active prototype development phase. These developments have taken place in several areas, for example:

-- Hardware is getting smaller, cheaper, and more powerful. Programming languages such as LISP (18) enable us to deal with A.I. concepts. In addition, the concepts, tools, and techniques for knowledge engineering - the work involved in capturing and codifying the knowledge of an expert - are beginning to be understood. A.I. research has always been characterized by its need for large amounts of computing resources. As the cost of hardware becomes irrelevant to the economics of problem solution, the techniques of A.I. are becoming more economically viable.

-- As companies begin to install global communications networks of either the broad or narrow band varieties, possibilities abound for the collection and interpretation of data. In some organizations, this development will provide the potential for enhanced decision making and the opportunity for effective use of A.I. techniques.

-- The recent proliferation of firms offering specialized A.I. services has resulted in the creation of new software and an increasingly large group of knowledge engineers. Some have started companies and are hiring and training people who are focussing on business applications. (See 3.)

The second question facing managers is the one of where to start. One possible area for initial experimentation is the productive use of an organization's assets. In what looks to be a decade of low growth, it will be essential to acquire and use assets astutely. Digital Equipment Corporation's use of an Expert System for "equipment configuration control" is one example. A second sensible place in which to begin using A.I. is in those areas in which the organization stands to gain a distinct competitive advantage. Schlumberger would seem to feel that their E.S. used as a drilling advisor is one such example. It is interesting that of the more than 20 organizations personally known to the authors to be investing in work in E.S. and E.S.S. almost none would allow themselves to be quoted. The reasons given basically boiled down to the fact that they were experimenting with prototypes that they were expecting to give them a competitive advantage in making or delivering their product or service. Examples of this where we can quote without attribution are cases such as an E.S.S. for supporting the cross selling of financial services products, such as an insurance salesman selling a tax shelter. In another case it is the desire of a financial services organization to evaluate the credit worthiness of a loan applicant.

It is clear that there are a great many problem areas where even our somewhat primitive ability to deal with E.S. can permit the building of useful first generation systems. With E.S.S. the situation is even brighter as any help we can provide the beleaguered 'expert' will provide leverage for the organization.

The Problems, Risks and Issues

It would be irresponsible to conclude this article without commenting on the fact that Expert Systems and Expert Support Systems are in their infancy, and researchers and users alike must be realistic about the capabilities of these new systems. One risk, already apparent, is that the expert systems will be poorly defined and oversold, and the resulting backlash will hinder progress. It can be argued that the Western economies lost the most recent round on the economic battlefield to Japan, due in part to their failure to manage productivity and quality as well as their inability to select the markets in which they wished to excel. We face a similar risk with Expert Systems and their applications, and if we are careless we will lose out in exploiting this particular potential of the information era.

There is this danger of proceeding too quickly, too recklessly, without paying careful attention to what we are doing. One example is that we may well embed our knowledge (necessarily incomplete at any moment in time) into a system that is effective when used by the person who created it. When this same system is used by others, however, there is a risk of misapplication, holes in another user's knowledge could represent a pivotal element in the logic leading to a solution. While these holes are implicitly recognized by the creator of the knowledge base, they may be quite invisible to a new user of the knowledge base.

The challenge of proceeding at an appropriate pace can be met if managers treat the subject of Artificial Intelligence, Expert Systems, Expert Support Systems, and Decision Support Systems as a serious topic which will require management attention if it is to be exploited properly. Managers must recognize the differences between Type I and II problems, for which the older techniques are appropriate, and the new methods available for Types III and IV.

CONCLUSIONS

There are, then, some basic risks and constraints which will be with us for some time. However, the potential of A.I. techniques are obvious, and if we proceed cautiously, acknowledging the problems, we can begin to achieve worthwhile results.

The illustrations used here are merely two of some fifteen or twenty that have been described in some detail (see Bibliography) and have been built in a relatively brief period of time with primitive tools. This is a start-up phase for Expert Systems and Expert Support Systems, Phase Zero. Business has attempted to develop expert systems applications since 1980 and, despite the enormity of some of the problems, has succeeded in developing a number of simple and powerful prototypes.

The state of the art is such that everyone building an expert system must endure this primitive start-up phase in order to learn what is involved in this fascinating new field. We expect that it will take until about 1990 for E.S. and E.S.S. to be fully recognized as having achieved worthwhile business results.

However Expert Systems and Expert Support Systems are with us
now, albeit in a primitive form. The challenge for management is to
harness these tools to increase the effectiveness of the
organization and thus add value for its stakeholders. The
pioneering firms are leading the way, once a section of territory
has been staked out, the experience gained by these leaders will be
hard to equal. The time to examine the options carefully is now.

FOOTNOTES

1. Alexander, T., "The Next Revolution in Computer Programming, *Fortune*, October 29, 1984, pp. 81-86.

2. Anthony, R.N., "Planning and Control Systems: A Framework for Analysis," Boston: Harvard University Graduate School of Business Administration, 1965.

3. *Business Week*, "Artificial Intelligence: The second computer age begins," March 3, 1982.

4. Bachant, J., and McDermott, J., "R1 Revisited: Four years in the Trenches," AI Magazine, Fall, 1984. pp. 21-32.

5. Davis R., Austin, H., Carlborn, I., Frawley, B., Pruchnik, P., Sneiderman, R., Gilreath, J.A., "The Dipmeter Advisor: Interpretation of Geological Signals, *Proceedings of the 7th International Joint Conference on Artificial Intelligence*, Vancouver, Canada: 1981, pp. 846-849.

6. *Fortune*, "Teaching Computers the Art of Reason," May 17, 1982, and "Computers on the Road to Self-Improvement," June 14, 1982.

7. Fox, M.S., "Constraint-directed Search: A Case Study of Job-Shop Scheduling, Carnegie-Mellon University Robotics Institute, Technical Report No CMU-RI-TR-83-22, Pittsburgh, Pennsylvania: 1983.

8. Gorry, Anthony, and Michael S. Scott Morton, "A Framework for Management Information Systems," Sloan Management Review, Massachusetts Institute of Technology, Vol. 13, No. 1, Fall 1971.

9. Hayes-Roth, Frederick, Donald A. Waterman, Douglas B. Lenat, Editors, *Building Expert Systems*, Addison-Wesley Publ. Co, Inc., 1983.

10. Hollan, J.D., Hutchins, E.L. & Weitzman, L., "Steamer: An Interactive, Inspectable Simulation-based Training System," AI Magazine, Summer, 984, pp. 15-28.

11. Keen, Peter, and Michael S. Scott Morton, *Decision Support Systems: An Organizational Perspective*, Reading, Massachusetts: Addison-Wesley Publishing Company, Inc., 1978.

12. McDermott, John, "R1: A Rule-Based Configurer of Computer Systems," _Artificial Intelligence_, Vol. 19, No. 1, 1982.

13. Newell, A., "Reasoning: Problem solving, and decision processes: The Problem space as a fundamental category. In R. Nickerson (Ed.) _Attention and Performance VIII_, Hillsdale, N.J.: Erlbaum, 1980.

14. B. Sheil, "Power Tools for Programmers," _Datamation_, February, 1983, pp. 131-144.

15. Simon, Herbert A., _The New Science of Management Decision_, N.Y. Harper & Row, 1960.

16. Winston, Patrick Henry, _Artificial Intelligence_, 2nd Ed., Addison-Wesley Publ. Co., Inc., 1984, 1977.

17. Winston, _supra_, p. 88, 132-134.

18. Hayes-Roth, _supra_, Chs. 5, 6, 9.

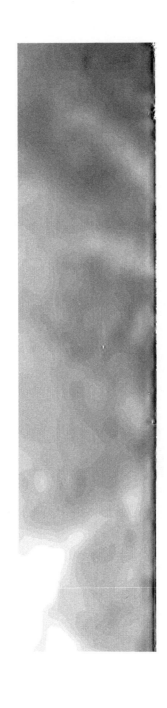

Lightning Source UK Ltd.
Milton Keynes UK
UKHW020047220421
382415UK00011B/157